Talk about the people at the front of the picture. Who do you think they are? What are they doing? Is there anything amusing or out of place about the things they are wearing or doing? Look at the people further away. Is there anything that makes you laugh or that seems strange? Look carefully at the rest of the picture. Is there anything unusual or not quite right? Ask pupils to make **b** sound. Point out things that begin with **b** sound.

1

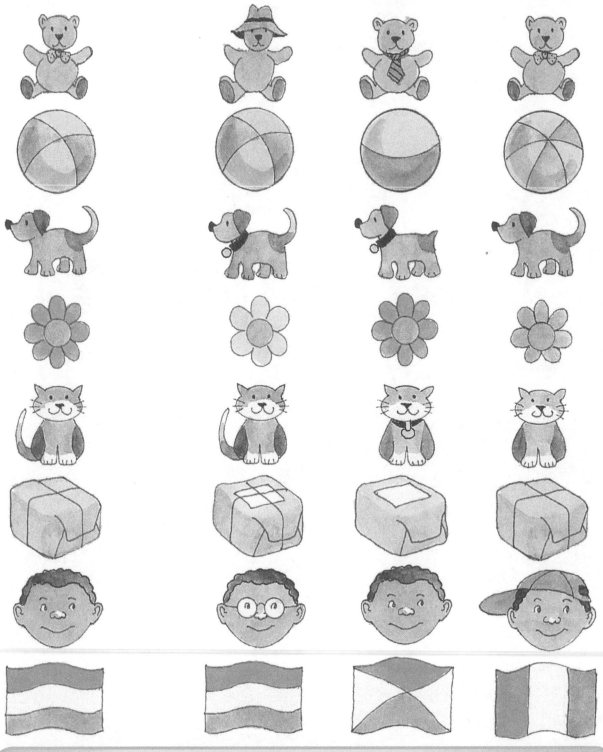

Help pupils discuss each set of pictures on the right. Talk about similarities and differences in shapes, colours, patterns, etc., within each set. Ask pupils to match the picture on the left with the identical one on the right. Revise **b** sound. Let pupils point out things that begin with **b** sound. Do drill with teacher and pupils pointing to items on the page that begin with **b** sound, e.g., *Teacher:* What is it? *Pupils*: It is a boy. *Teacher:* What is it? *Pupils*: It is a ball. *Teacher:* What is it? *Pupils*: It is a bear. Make the drill fun by doing it rhythmically.

What do pupils think each picture is? Pupils will recognize the planet, a star, a rocket (or space ship), the moon and the sun. Let them say what they know about the movement of the Earth, space, planets, stars, space shuttles, etc. Ask them to trace each shape with their index finger several times. Let pupils copy the shapes if they wish, and colour them. Ask them to tell stories about space travel. Help them make up stories and draw pictures to illustrate them.

Talk about each picture. Let pupils name each creature and say what they know about it. Do a quick drill to revise "What is it? It is a...", e.g., *Teacher:* What is it? *Pupils:* It is a goat. *Teacher:* What is it? *Pupils:* It is a pig. Have them match the pictures. (There are eight pairs.) Put each pair together in any order to tell a short story, e.g., "The dog sat up and begged for a bone. He barked 'Woof!' to say thanks, and then he went off to gnaw on it." Help pupils to make up a story for each pair of pictures. Let them be as imaginative as they wish.

Ask pupils to name each creature. Talk about where each is going and why. (Remember, this is an open-ended discussion. Even unusual answers are fine.) Ask pupils to trace over each dotted line several times with their index fingers. (These patterns are the basis for the formation of many letters.) Let pupils practise the patterns by making them on the desk with their index fingers, or writing them on the CB or WB. They can also make them on sheets of paper with pencils, felt tip pens or paint.

5

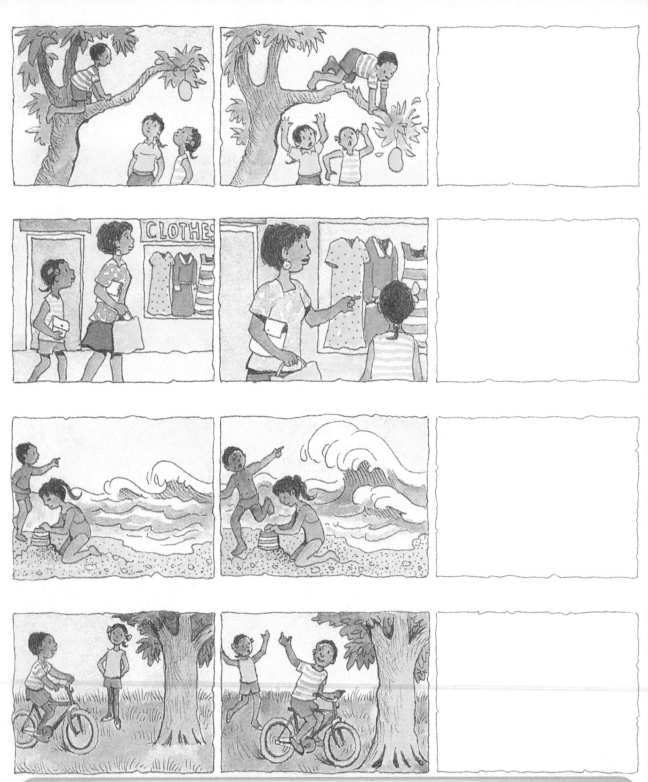

6 Each pair of pictures tells part of a story. Talk about the pictures in detail, one pair at a time. Let pupils be creative. They can make up names for the people in the pictures, e.g., Sandra, Betty, Roy, and describe them, as well as the places where each story takes place, e.g., Boston Beach, Mango Walk, etc. Let pupils tell each story, making up what people say and think. Ask them what they think happens next. Have them draw the last picture(s), showing the endings they choose.

Pupils trace over dotted lines in the fence with their index fingers several times. Point out that these are straight lines that go up and down. Let pupils talk about each object, naming it, saying how big it is, what it is used for, etc. Let them use their index fingers to trace the dotted lines in the shape of each letter. Repeat the name of each item, stressing the initial sound: **key**. Repeat the sound, saying the name again, e.g., **k, k, k, key**. Let pupils repeat after you. Do this for each picture. Let pupils think of other things starting with **l, k, d, t, f**.

Pupils take turns naming and talking about the objects. You may need to help them with some names, e.g., the **pan sticks** are used to play the steel pan. Let them put the objects in pairs: glove and hand, knife and fork, etc. If they make unusual suggestions, let them give reasons, and talk about whether the explanations make sense, e.g., Can glove and paint go together, if you wear gloves while you paint? Can shoe and glove go together, since you wear both? Ask them to think of other pairs of things. Let them draw some pairs.

red   green   blue   yellow   brown

Let pupils talk about the picture. Who are the people in the picture? Where are they going? How can you tell? Ask about what each person will do with the things they are carrying. Ask pupils to name the colours in the paint box. Let them find objects in the picture with each of these colours. Ask them to name the colours of things in the classroom and things they can see outside. Let them paint or colour a picture of their choice.

9

Pupils trace over dotted lines for the rain with their index fingers several times. Tell them the lines are **vertical** lines, i.e. they go directly up and down. Let pupils talk about objects. Let them name each object and use their fingers to trace the dotted lines in the shape of each letter. Name each picture for the pupils, stressing the initial sound, e.g., **pen**. Repeat the sound, saying the name again. e.g., **p, p, p, pen**. Let pupils repeat. Do this for each picture and initial letter sound. Let pupils think of other things starting with **i, j, n, p**.

Pupils look at the top half of page and name the animals that would be formed by putting the jigsaw pieces together. Talk about each of the animals. What noise does it make? What does it eat? Is it a **wild** or **domestic** animal? Where is it kept? Is it used for anything? Let pupils look at the bottom half of the page. Explain that part of each creature is missing. Ask them to identify each one. Let them draw and colour any of the animals shown on the page, or any other animal they choose.

Have pupils look quietly at each of the two sets of pictures, then let them talk about what is happening in each picture *in the first set*. Explain that the pictures tell a story but that they are in the wrong order. Let them say what the correct order should be and let them tell the story. Ask them what they think happens next. Then ask them to give the story a title. Discuss the second set of pictures in the same way, repeating the activities. Let them draw a picture in their books that illustrates the end of one of the stories.

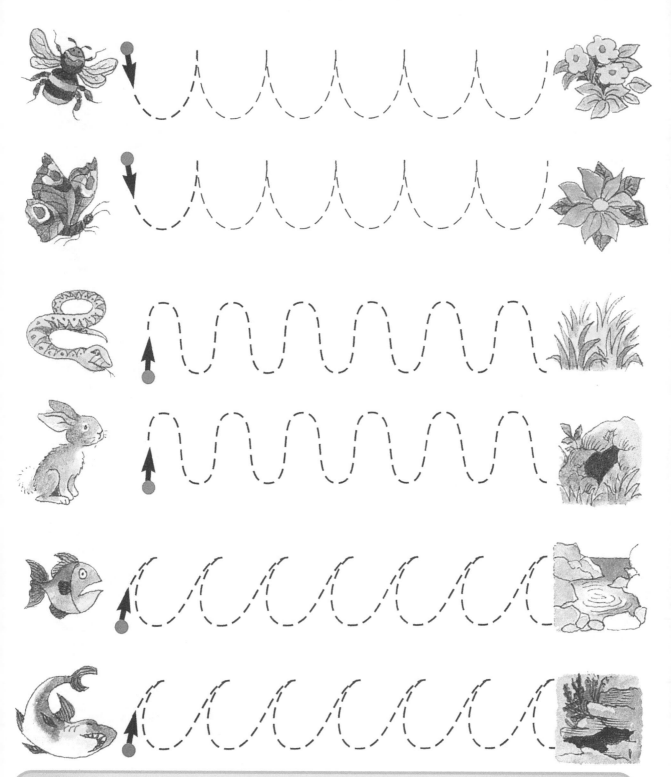

Let pupils name and talk about each creature, then ask them: Where is the bee/butterfly/snake/rabbit/fish/shark going? Why is it going to that place? (If they need help, explain that the shark is going to an undersea cave.) Pupils trace over dotted lines several times with their index fingers. Let pupils practise the patterns by making them on the desk with their index fingers or writing them on the CB or WB. They can also make them on paper with pencil, felt tip pens or paint.

13

Ask pupils to name and talk about each creature shown: where it lives, what it eats, how it moves, etc. Let pupils compare shapes of creatures and identify the ones that are similar, e.g., crab and spider; shark and crocodile. Help them with words like **fin, claw, whiskers, gills, fangs**, if need be. Discuss characteristics of the shadows (or silhouettes) of each, e.g., long tails of some animals; short tails of others. Look for clues in each shape e.g., crab's claws, rabbit's whiskers. Ask pupils to match each shape to the correct animal.

Talk about frogs: where they live, how they move, etc. Let pupils trace over the dotted line leading to the pond with their index fingers. Let pupils talk about the pictures. Let them identify each and use their fingers to trace the dotted lines in the shape of each letter. Name each picture for them again, stressing the initial sound, e.g., **bat**. Repeat the sound and the name, e.g., **b, b, b, bat**. Let pupils repeat. Do this for each picture. Let pupils think of other things starting with **b, r, h, m**. Work with pupils who have difficulty hearing and saying letter **h**.

15

Let pupils trace the shapes 'in the sea' with their index fingers. Talk about different shapes. Use the words **circle**, **round**, **square**, **triangle**, **cross**, **diamond**, **star**, making sure they understand the meanings. Point out the difference between a cross and the letter **t**. Ask pupils to match each shape with its partner 'on the sand'. Talk about colours of each shape. Let them count, e.g., all the shapes with straight sides, all the red shapes, etc. Let pupils draw shapes on the CB/WB or in their books, make and colour pictures containing the shapes, etc.

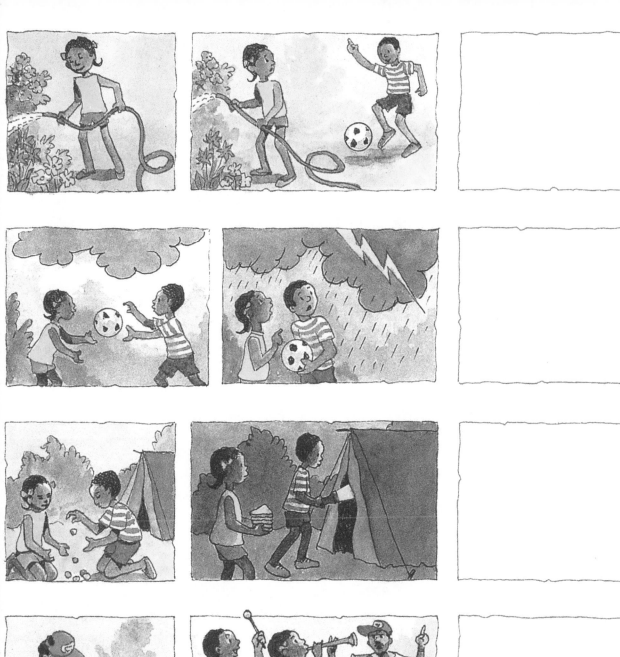

Explain that each set of pictures tells a story and have pupils look quietly at each set. Let pupils talk about what is happening in the pictures, taking each set in turn. Ask them what they think happens next in each case and let them tell the story for each set. (Different children will have stories that end in different ways.) Then ask them to give each story a title. Let them draw, colour or paint the picture that illustrates the end of one of the stories in their books.

Talk about items in each line, discussing similarities and differences. Point out the variety of items in line five. Look at the first line. Name the item on the left, stressing initial **m** sound. Repeat **m** sound, and then say the name again. Let pupils name items on right and find the one starting with **m** sound. Repeat for each line. Look at the snake at the bottom of the page. Ask pupils to say **snake**. Repeat the word for them, stressing **s** sound. Ask them to find things in the classroom starting with **s** sound. (Some pupils may need individual help with **s** sound.)

Talk about what the children at the top of page are doing. Ask pupils to trace over the dotted lines that show the path of the ball with their index fingers. Let pupils talk about each object shown, saying how big it is, what it is used for, etc. Let them use their index fingers to trace the dotted lines in the shape of each letter. Repeat the name of each item, stressing the initial sound: **van**. Repeat the sound, saying the name again, e.g., **v, v, v, van**. Let pupils repeat after you. Do this for each picture. Let pupils think of other words starting with **v, x, y, w, z**.

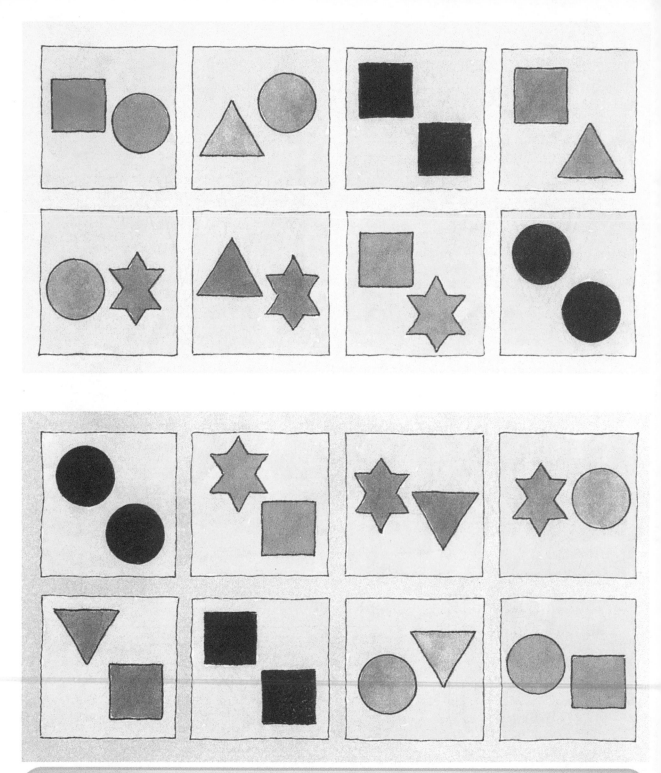

Talk about the shapes at top of page, revising the words **circle**, **round**, **square**, **triangle**, **star**. Let pupils trace the shapes with their index fingers. Let pupils name each pair of shapes and identify the colour of each pair. Then ask pupils to match each pair of coloured shapes at the top of the page with the same pair at the bottom. (Point out positions of shapes may be different, but that the pairs should be the same.) Let pupils count: all the blue/green/red/black shapes; all the stars; all the circles, etc.

the car

the mat

the bed

the box

the box   the bed   the car   the mat

a hat   a cat   a hat on a cat

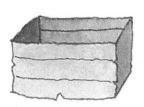  

a box   a fox

a wig   a pig

 a frog

Talk about the pictures in the first line. What kind of hat is this? What do you think it's made of? Talk about the expression on the cat's face. Remind pupils that the writing underneath says the name of each thing. Ask them to make up a rhyme with the words **hat** and **cat**. Tell them that the words under the last picture say: **a hat on a cat**. Talk about the rhyme. Ask them to make up other rhymes with **cat** and **hat**. Do this for each line. Talk about frogs. Help pupils to make rhymes with **frog**. Have fun saying these rhymes and any others they know.

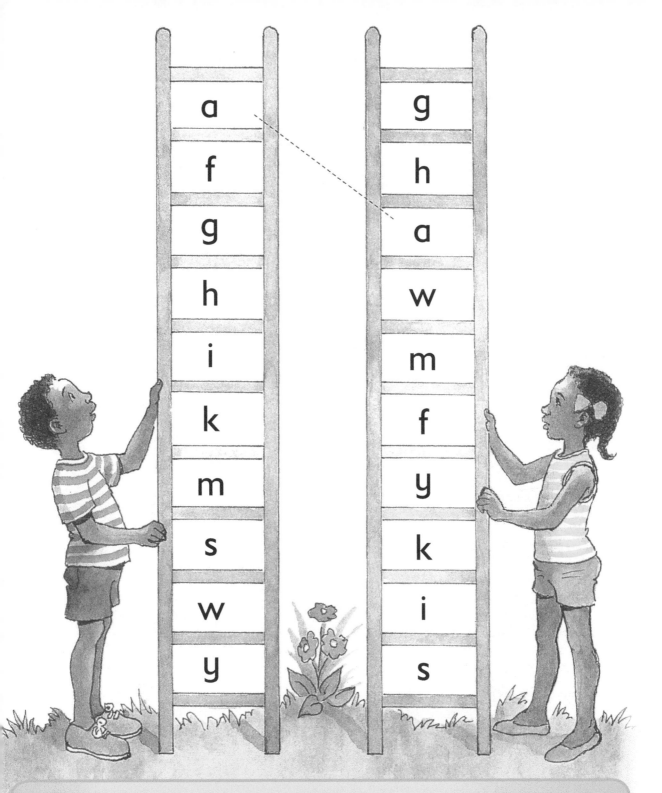

Tell pupils the names of the children: the boy's name is Colin and the girl's name is Pam. Ask pupils what they think Colin and Pam are doing. Holding up the ladders? Reading the letters? Then ask them to help Colin and Pam to say and sound the letters on each ladder, going from top to bottom, then from bottom to top. Let pupils match the letters. If they have difficulty, revise the letter shapes, and revise the names and sounds of the letters.

23

Working one line at a time, let pupils talk about items shown. Say the name of the item on the left, stressing the initial letter sound: **fish**. Repeat the sound and the word, e.g., **f**, **f**, **f**, **fish**. Let pupils repeat the sound and the word. Ask them to name the three objects on the right and find the one that begins with the same sound. Look at the picture of the television. Ask pupils to say what it is. Repeat the word for them, stressing the initial letter sound. Ask pupils to find other things beginning with the same sound.

Ask pupils what the dotted line at the top of the page shows. Let them trace over it with their index fingers several times. Ask them to name each picture, using their fingers to trace the dotted lines in the shape of the letters **a**, **g**, **o**, **c**. Talk about any similarity in letter shapes. Name each picture for the pupils, stressing the initial sound, e.g., <u>c</u>rocodile. Say the sound several times and repeat the name, e.g., **c, c, c,** <u>c</u>rocodile. Ask pupils to repeat. Repeat for each picture. Let pupils think of other things starting with **a**, **g**, **o**, **c**.

Have pupils look quietly at each of the two sets of pictures, then let them talk about what each picture *in the first set* shows. Explain that the pictures tell a story but that they are in the wrong order. Let them say what the correct order should be and let them tell the story. Ask them what they think might happen to continue the story. Let them give the story a title. Discuss the second set of pictures in the same way, repeating the activities. Let them draw the picture that shows what happens next in one or both of the stories.

Colin   Pam   Mummy   Daddy

M P
C D

Let pupils talk about Colin, Pam, Mummy and Daddy. Let them sound the initial letters in the words written below each picture. Remind pupils that the writing underneath says what each picture is. Ask them to say whose name begins with each of the letters in the middle of the page. Explain that the pictures at the bottom of the page are torn. Let pupils find the parts that go together. Let them name the person in each reconstructed picture and take turns writing the initial letters in each name on the CB or WB, or let them write the letters in their books.

a bug   **a mug**   **a bug in a mug**

a pen   **a hen**

 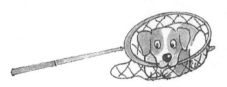

a net   **a pet**

a sock   **a clock**

Pam

28

Talk about all the pictures, and then look back at those in the first line. Ask pupils what the writing under each picture says. If necessary, help them to read it. Let pupils point to and say, **a bug** and **a mug**, then ask them to say what the picture on the right is. Tell them the words under the picture say **a bug in a mug**. Talk about the rhyme. Ask pupils to make up another rhyme with **mug** and **bug**, e.g., **a mug with a bug**. Do this for each line. Help them to make rhymes with the word **Pam**. Have fun saying these rhymes and any others they know.

Pam

Daddy

Amrita

Colin

Mummy

Mummy Amrita Colin Pam Daddy

Let pupils talk about flying kites on a windy day. What do most kites have attached that none of these kites have? Ask pupils to trace the strings to each of the kites with their index fingers to find out who is holding them. (You may have to help some pupils sound out the names on the kites.) One person is holding the kite with their name on it. Who? (Mummy.) Who is holding each of the other kites? Do a drill, e.g., *Teacher:* Is Pam's kite high? *Pupils:* Yes. Pam's kite is high. *Teacher:* Is Colin's kite high? *Pupils:* No. Colin's kite is low. And so on.

Ask pupils what the dotted line at the top of the page shows. Let them trace over it with their index fingers several times. Ask them to name each picture, using their fingers to trace the dotted lines in the shape of the letters **q, u, e, s**. Name each picture for the pupils, stressing the initial sound e.g., **u**mbrella. Say the sound several times and say the name again, e.g., **u, u, u, u**mbrella. Ask pupils to repeat. Do this for each picture and initial letter sound. Ask pupils to think of other things starting with **q, u, e, s**.

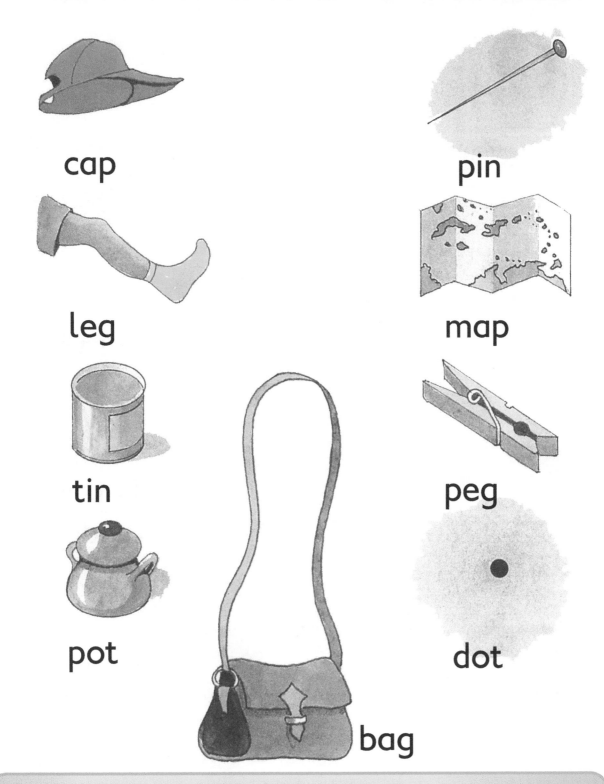

cap

pin

leg

map

tin

peg

pot

dot

bag

Talk about each of the items in the picture. Ask pupils whether some things have other names, e.g., a **tin** is sometimes a **can**; a clothes **peg** is sometimes called a clothes **pin**; a **dot** can also be a **spot**, etc. Remind pupils that the writing underneath says the name of each thing. Match up words and pictures that rhyme. Talk some more about the bag. How is it worn? What could it be made of? Ask pupils to think of other words that rhyme with **bag**.

31

Colin   **Pam**   **Mummy**   **Daddy**

 Is this Colin?

 Is this Pam?

 Is this Mummy?

 Is this Daddy?

 Is this Colin?

 Is this Pam?